GERONIMO

APACHE WARRIOR

SPECIAL LIVES IN HISTORY THAT BECOME

Signature LIVES

GERONIMO

APACHE WARRIOR

by Brenda Haugen

Content Adviser: Liz Sonneborn,
Author, The American West

*Reading Adviser: Rosemary G. Palmer, Ph.D.,
Department of Literacy, College of Education,
Boise State University*

COMPASS POINT BOOKS MINNEAPOLIS, MINNESOTA

Compass Point Books
3109 West 50th Street, #115
Minneapolis, MN 55410

Visit Compass Point Books on the Internet at *www.compasspointbooks.com*
or e-mail your request to *custserv@compasspointbooks.com*

Editor: Editorial Directions, Inc.
Lead Designer: Jaime Martens
Photo Researcher: Marcie C. Spence
Cartographer: XNR Productions, Inc.
Educational Consultant: Diane Smolinski

Managing Editor: Catherine Neitge
Creative Director: Keith Griffin
Editorial Director: Carol Jones

To Kevin Jeffrey, for putting up with more than he ever should! BLH

Library of Congress Cataloging-in-Publication Data
Haugen, Brenda.
  Geronimo : Apache warrior / by Brenda Haugen.
     p. cm. — (Signature lives)
  Includes bibliographical references and index.
  ISBN 0-7565-1002-3 (hard cover)
  1. Geronimo, 1829–1909—Juvenile literature. 2. Apache Indians—Kings
and rulers—Biography—Juvenile literature. 3. Apache Indians—Wars—
Juvenile literature. I. Title. II. Series.
  E99.A6G474 2006
  979.004'9725'0092—dc22   2005005693

Signature Lives

AMERICAN FRONTIER ERA

By the late 1700s, the United States was growing into a nation of homesteaders, politicians, mountain men, and American dreams. Manifest Destiny propelled settlers to push west, conquering and "civilizing" from coast to coast. In keeping with this vision, world leaders hammered out historic agreements such as the Louisiana Purchase, which drastically increased U.S. territory. This ambition often led to bitter conflicts with Native Americans trying to protect their way of life and their traditional lands. Life on the frontier was often filled with danger and difficulties. The people who wove their way into American history overcame these challenges with a courage and conviction that defined an era and shaped a nation.

Table of Contents

Chapter
1 MASSACRE

༺◦⬧◦༻

Geronimo's face contorted with grief and anger. He returned to camp from a trip to Janos, Mexico, and found his mother, Juana, his wife, Alope, and his children slaughtered. Geronimo's family members were among the many people killed mercilessly by Mexicans who attacked the small, riverside camp. A few warriors had stayed behind to guard the women and children, but they, too, had been killed.

The Mexicans were led by Colonel Jose Maria Carrasco, who believed Geronimo and the other Apache he lived with had been raiding the Mexican state of Sonora. Carrasco saw all Apache people as wild murderers and robbers and needed little excuse to seek revenge. As commander of Sonora's military, Carrasco took about 400 of his men into the

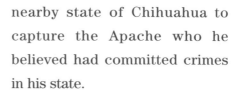

nearby state of Chihuahua to capture the Apache who he believed had committed crimes in his state.

The people in Chihuahua lived in peace with the Apache camped near Janos. Leaders of the two groups had signed a treaty on June 24, 1850, and Chihuahuan officials believed the Apache people had lived up to their side of the bargain. They doubted the Sonoran officials' story that these Apache had murdered and robbed people. In fact, the Sonorans were probably right. It's likely that Geronimo and the other Apache had been involved in the raids in Sonora.

But officials from Chihuahua had spent a great deal of money on rations and other supplies to keep the Apache from raiding their cities. The Apache usually raided only out of desperation—to find enough supplies to survive when times proved tough. The Chihuahuan officials didn't want the Sonorans to ruin the peace and stir up trouble.

Carrasco continued with his plans, however, with little regard for what the truth may have been or what the feelings of the people in Chihuahua were. Believing there was no such thing as a peaceful Apache, Carrasco ordered his men to attack the Apache camp where Geronimo lived on March 5, 1851.

Before the attack, most of the Apache men—including Geronimo—had headed to town. Not expecting any trouble, the men believed their families would be safe with the warriors left behind as guards. But trouble was marching straight toward the Apache camp. Seeing the soldiers, the women and children tried to flee, but it was too late. More than 20 Apache people were killed in the massacre, and another 62 were captured.

As Geronimo and the others made their way back toward camp, they learned the news:

> *Late one afternoon when returning from town we were met by a few women and children who told us that Mexican troops from some other town had attacked our camp, killed all the warriors of the guard, captured all our ponies, secured our arms, destroyed our supplies, and killed many of our women and children. Quickly we separated, concealing ourselves as best we could until nightfall, when we assembled at our appointed place of rendezvous—a thicket by the river. Silently we stole in one by one, sentinels were placed, and when all were counted, I found that my aged mother, my young wife, and my three small children were among the slain.*

Geronimo's heart was broken. He would never be the same again.

As he watched the other Apache leave for Arizona, Geronimo felt lost as to what he should do. "I had no weapon, nor did I hardly wish to fight, neither did I contemplate recovering the bodies of my loved ones, for that was forbidden," Geronimo said.

Chihuahua is the largest state in Mexico. It borders the U.S. states of New Mexico and Texas and was once home to many Apache.

The loss of his family led Geronimo to a lifelong hatred of all Mexicans. Consumed with sadness and rage, Geronimo swore revenge—and he would accomplish it many times over. He became one of

the most feared Apache warriors of all time.

Geronimo and other Apache raiders looted, burned, and murdered their way through Arizona and New Mexico as they made

Indians captured in Mexico during the mid-1800s were often sold into slavery.

their way back and forth across the border separating the United States and Mexico. Newspapers whipped up fear among their readers with stories of savage attacks made by the Apache. Some of the stories stuck to the truth, while many articles proved false. Throughout the United States and Mexico, Geronimo was blamed for far more destruction and death than he ever sowed. The articles served to make Geronimo a well-known and feared man.

The fame, however, only made a tough situation worse for the Apache. In the middle to late 1880s, the Apache found themselves in an increasingly difficult spot. To the south, some Mexican authorities wanted all the Apache people killed. To the north, America's westward expansion affected the Apache, too, forcing them off their land. Nearly as quickly as the United States government made promises of reservation land for the Apache, the promises would be broken. An area rich in resources, Apache land in the southwestern United States held deposits of precious minerals.

A group of Apache attacks a U.S. government surveying party in 1852. The Apache often clashed with the white people who were taking over their lands.

Once silver, copper, and other resources were found, the land was gobbled up by those coming west to seek their fortunes—whether the ground belonged to the Apache or not.

Geronimo would be forced to live on a reservation several times, but he found it difficult. He would eventually find a reason to break out and head for the mountains of Mexico. Part of the issue was freedom. Another part involved trust. Many branded Geronimo a liar, but many of the white people he dealt with proved untrustworthy, too. After being pursued and captured, and escaping again, Geronimo eventually surrendered for the final time.

Again the promises made to him were broken, and he and his friends and family were imprisoned and separated. Disease ravaged his people, but while loved ones died, the strong, tough Geronimo persevered.

Though he remained a captive the rest of his life, Geronimo also became a legend. Geronimo became an attraction at fairs and exhibitions where people flocked to see him. He even rode in a Washington, D.C., parade at the request of a president.

Yet until the day he died, Geronimo never stopped trying to gain his freedom and find his way back to the homeland where he'd spent his happiest days.

Silver stands as one of the first metals ever used by humans. As early as 4000 B.C., people not only used silver for money but wore jewelry made from it. Today, the United States ranks second, only behind Mexico, in silver production. The states that lead production of the precious metal include Nevada, Idaho, and Arizona.

Chapter

2 GROWING UP

‿⟡‿

Geronimo claimed to have been born in June 1829. The Apache didn't keep track of days the way whites at the time did, so no one knows for sure when Geronimo came into the world. Named Goyakla by his parents, he would gain fame with the name Geronimo— a nickname he would earn battling Mexicans.

Though he'd never met his grandfather Mahko, Geronimo grew up listening to stories about this great man. Chief Mahko had served as the leader of the Bedonkohe Apache but died when Geronimo's father, Taklishim, was still a young warrior.

Taklishim loved to tell stories about war, history, and hunting, but some of his favorite stories involved his own father. Chief Mahko loved peace, and his generosity knew no end. He'd gladly share

> *Goyakla means "one who yawns." Taklishim means "the gray one."*

whatever he had with the less fortunate of his people. A big, strong man, Mahko was also remembered as a brave warrior who fought against the Mexicans.

Taklishim said, however, that Mahko only fought the Mexicans after he was first attacked.

Geronimo loved to listen to Taklishim's stories and dreamed of the day when he, too, would prove himself a great warrior. As a little boy, he practiced his warrior skills while playing with his friends:

> *Sometimes we played that we were warriors. We would practice stealing up on some object that represented the enemy, and in our childish imitation often performed the feats of war. Sometimes we would hide from our mother to see if she could find us, and often when thus concealed go to sleep and perhaps remain hidden for many hours.*

Geronimo enjoyed his mother's stories, too. Juana's tales told the stories of the Apache people. She also taught Geronimo and his sister how to pray to the Life Giver, sometimes called Usen:

> *When a child my mother taught me the legends of our people; taught me of the sun and sky, the moon and stars, the clouds*

and storms. She also taught me to kneel and pray to Usen for strength, health, wisdom, and protection. We never prayed against any person, but if we had aught against any individual we ourselves took vengeance. We were taught that Usen does not care for the petty quarrels of men.

The Apache often lived in dome-shaped huts known as wickiups.

Life wasn't all stories and fun, though. As a young boy, Geronimo went with his mother and the other women to gather nuts and berries. Bears also loved the sweet treats, so care had to be taken to stay safe. Geronimo learned this lesson after one woman strayed from the rest of the group. No one noticed she was missing until her pony showed up back at the camp. Still loaded with her baskets, the pony wasn't carrying its rider.

Several Apache went out looking for the woman and eventually found her. She had been attacked by a bear but had been able to fight back. As her dog snapped at the growling creature, the woman had stabbed the bear several times, and it ran away. She was badly injured, but the camp's medicine man was skilled in the use of healing herbs and nursed her back to health.

An Apache hunter collects rattlesnake venom using a deer liver for bait. Rattlesnake venom can be used as poison on arrows.

> *The Indians knew what herbs to use for medicine, how to prepare them, and how to give the medicine. This they had been*

taught by Usen from the beginning. In gathering the herbs, in preparing them, and in administering the medicine, as much faith was held in prayer as in the actual effect of the medicine.

Geronimo also learned about using herbs for medicine and became skilled at removing bullets and arrowheads from warriors injured in battle. Some even considered him a medicine man in his adulthood. But before that time came, Geronimo worked with his father and learned to be a farmer.

When we were old enough to be of real service we went to the field with our parents: not to play, but to toil. When the crops were planted we broke the ground with wooden hoes. We planted the corn in straight rows, the beans among the corn, and the melons and pumpkins in irregular order over the field.

The crops would help feed the family throughout the year.

Melons were gathered as they were consumed. In the autumn pumpkins and beans were gathered and placed in bags or baskets; ears of corn were tied together by the husks, and then the harvest was carried on the backs of ponies up to our homes. Here the corn was shelled, and the

An Apache chief (left), medicine man, and war chief

harvest stored away in caves or other secluded places to be used in the winter.

Like other Apache, Geronimo learned to hide as well as fight. Their safety often depended on their ability to cover their tracks and hide in the many caves and crevices that the mountains and the rest of the countryside provided them. Apache children played hiding games. The skills they developed through play might someday save their lives, so they were never chastised for it.

Frequently when the tribe was in camp a number of boys and girls, by agreement, would steal away and meet at a place sev-

eral miles distant, where they could play all day free from tasks. They were never punished for these frolics; but if their hiding places were discovered they were ridiculed.

The Apache loved their children, and Geronimo's family was no exception. Though he had only one sister, Nah-dos-te, Geronimo considered many of his cousins to be his brothers and sisters, too.

Geronimo and his family lived in a home that was fashioned from antelope and deer hides. The side with hair faced the outdoors, helping to keep the home waterproof. Their lives were relatively peaceful. Whites had not yet invaded their country. "During my minority we had never seen a missionary or a priest," Geronimo said. "We had never seen a white man. Thus quietly lived the Be-don-ko-he Apaches."

Up until age 5 or 6, boys and girls played together. After that, men began teaching the boys, and women instructed the girls. The girls helped with tasks such as carrying water and collecting wood. They also learned to cook and make clothes.

An Apache woman poses with baskets she has made. Basket making was just one of the many skills taught to Apache girls.

Many different kinds of wildlife were found in the area where Geronimo grew up. The men of the tribe hunted cougars, deer, antelope, eagles, and elk. The Apache also hunted buffalo, though they were more diffi-cult to find. Buffalo hides were used as bed-ding and as coverings for Apache homes.

Boys learned to care for the group's horses and make weapons and tools. They practiced shooting bows and arrows and prepared to become warriors.

As soon as Geronimo proved he could handle a bow and arrows, he learned to hunt small animals. Most boys started hunt-ing bigger game with the men when they were about 14, but it is likely that Geronimo began hunt-ing bigger game between the ages of 8 and 10. He showed great skill in making and using weapons.

The Apache knew how to have fun when their work was done. They enjoyed getting together to celebrate a successful hunt or other special event. "I was always glad when the dances and the feasts were announced," Geronimo remembered. "So were all the other young people."

Tragedy struck Geronimo's household when he was still young. His father died after a long illness. Taklishim was buried in a cave with his possessions. This was the Apache burial custom. The Apache believed a person's belongings went with him or her into the next world. The cave's entrance was then sealed with rocks. Mud was slathered on the rocks to fill in the spaces between them.

Also according to Apache custom, Geronimo now had to step up and become a man. "After my father's death I assumed the care of my mother," Geronimo said. His sister had already married and moved away from home. "My mother chose to live with me, and she never desired to marry again. We lived near our old home and I supported her."

Geronimo continued to dream of the day when he would become a great warrior. He got his chance in 1846 after he turned 17. He became part of the council of warriors, which meant he could go into

A buffalo grazes on a grassy plain. The Apache hunted buffalo and many other animals.

The Sierra Madre reigns as the chief mountain system in Mexico. It is composed of three mountain ranges—the Sierra Madre Oriental, the Sierra Madre Occidental, and the Sierra Madre del Sur. At it highest point, the Sierra Madre stretches about 13,000 feet (3,965 meters) into the sky. Parts of the range include volcanic mountains.

battle with the other warriors. "This would be glorious," Geronimo said. "I hoped soon to serve my people in battle. I had long desired to fight with our warriors."

As a warrior, Geronimo now also earned the right to marry. He had loved a beautiful girl named Alope for a long time. She was a member of the Nednai band of Apache. They met when he was visiting his favorite cousin, Ishton, who was married to Juh, a Nednai who was one of Geronimo's best friends. The Nednai lived in the Sierra Madre, a mountain range in Mexico. Geronimo returned there with the intention of making Alope his wife.

Geronimo went to Alope's father to ask permission to marry her. The father asked for many horses in exchange for his daughter's hand in marriage. "I made no reply, but in a few days appeared before his [home] with the herd of ponies and took with me Alope," Geronimo recalled. "This was all the marriage ceremony necessary in our tribe." The newlyweds went to live among Geronimo's people, the Bedonkohe.

Not far from my mother's tepee I had made for us a new home. The tepee was made of buffalo hides and in it were many bear robes, [cougar] hides, and other trophies of the chase, as well as my spears, bows, and arrows. Alope had made many decorations of beads and drawn work on buckskin, which she placed in our tepee. She also drew many pictures on the walls of our room. She was a good wife, but she was never strong. We followed the traditions of our father and were happy. Three children came to us— children that played, loitered, and worked as I had done.

Life was good. Geronimo felt happy, but soon his life would change forever. ꙮ

3 TROUBLE IN MEXICO

Chapter

❧❧❧

For years, tension had been growing between the United States and Mexico. In 1835, Texas—then a part of Mexico—broke out on its own, forming the Republic of Texas the following year. Mexico did not recognize Texas' independence and warned the United States to steer clear of the argument.

Many people in the United States, however, believed in Manifest Destiny—the idea that their country would one day stretch all the way across North America, from the Atlantic to the Pacific oceans. Mexican land stood between the United States and this destiny.

Despite the warning from Mexico, the United States annexed Texas, which became a state in 1845. Mexico responded by breaking all diplomatic ties

The United States defeated Mexican forces at the Battle of Buena Vista on February 23, 1847.

with the United States. The disagreement grew, in part because of the United States' desire to seize more Mexican territory. Congress declared war against Mexico on May 13, 1846.

The Apache paid little attention to the fight between the two countries because they didn't believe it would affect them. But the Treaty of Guadalupe Hidalgo, which ended the war in 1848, forever changed the lives of these native people.

Under the treaty, the United States agreed to pay Mexico $15 million for the more than 525,000 square miles (1,365,000 square kilometers) of land that was at issue. Included in the deal were California, Utah, Nevada, parts of Colorado and Wyoming, and most of Arizona and New Mexico—places that Geronimo and his fellow Apache called home. Men surveying this land were among the first white people Geronimo ever encountered.

Today, the Rio Grande makes up about two-thirds of the boundary between the United States and Mexico.

We gave them buckskin, blankets, and ponies in exchange for shirts and provisions. We also brought them game, for which they gave us some money. We did not know the value of this money, but we kept it and later learned from the Navajo Indians that is was very valuable. Every day they measured land with curious instruments and put down marks which

*we could not understand. They were good
men, and we were sorry when they had
gone on into the west. They were not soldiers. These were the first white men I
ever saw.*

Along with paying Mexico for the land it gained,
the United States promised to help keep Indians

At the end of the Mexican War, the United States gained territory that eventually became the states of California, Utah, Nevada, parts of Colorado and Wyoming, and most of Arizona and New Mexico.

living on this land from attacking Mexican communities. This proved to be a difficult task.

Not all of the Apache lived in the United States. The Nednai, including Geronimo's friend Juh, lived in the Sierra Madres, which remained in Mexican territory. And as was customary with all Apache, the Nednai conducted raids when they ran low on supplies.

Chihuahuan officials had found that fighting the Apache not only proved costly, it didn't solve anything. They believed that if the Nednai had what they needed, they would cease their raids, and people in the communities could live unafraid. Hoping to make peace with the Nednai, the officials who governed this area invited the Nednai to trade in their communities and even set up a system for passing out rations and supplies.

The plan seemed to work. The Nednai traded animal hides and furs for cloth and tools. But sometimes they traded goods they'd stolen from another community. That is what Sonoran leader Colonel Jose Maria Carrasco believed was happening— Nednai were raiding Sonoran communities and trading the goods in Chihuahuan towns.

Other Apache heard of the trade agreement between the Chihuahuans and the Nednai. Mangas Coloradas, the leader of the Warm Springs band of Apache, decided to head south and take advantage of the trade agreement. Geronimo and several others joined Mangas on his adventure. Because the journey was planned as a peaceful trading mission, the Apache brought their families along, too.

Their destination was the Mexican city of Casas Grandes, but they planned a stay in Janos, Mexico, along the way. The government was scheduled to hand out supplies and gifts to the Apache in Janos,

Mangas, son of Apache leader Mangas Coloradas

and Mangas and his people wanted to be there when the goods were handed out.

Still wary of Mexicans, the Apache made camp outside of Janos. Each day, the Apache men traveled to town and picked up supplies, returning to camp at night. The women and children stayed behind at the camp guarded by a few warriors.

All went well for a while, but one evening as they returned to camp, the Apache men were met by a few of their women and children. Mexican soldiers led by Carrasco had attacked the camp, killing more than two dozen people, including Geronimo's family. Twice as many Apache had been captured.

The remaining Apache returned to their home along the Gila River. Geronimo was overwhelmed with anger and sadness.

Within a few days we arrived at our own settlement. There were the decorations that Alope had made—and there were the playthings of our little ones. I burned them all, even our tepee. I also burned my mother's tepee and destroyed all her property. I was never again contented in our quiet home. I had vowed vengeance upon the Mexican troopers who had wronged me, and whenever I ... saw anything to remind me of former happy days my heart would ache for revenge upon Mexico.

Native American Cultural Areas at Time of European Contact
- California
- Great Basin
- Great Plains
- Northeast
- Southeast
- Southwest

Tribal groups labeled in italic

After he burned all of his family's belongings, Geronimo went off alone and cried. As he mourned, he heard a voice calling his name. Though no one appeared, Geronimo listened as the voice continued speaking and brought him some comfort. "No gun can ever kill you," Geronimo heard the voice say. "I will take the bullets from the guns of the Mexicans, so they will have nothing but powder. And I will guide your arrows."

Mangas Coloradas called a war council to decide what the Apache should do to avenge the deaths of

Apache, like many Native American tribes, often traveled from place to place following herds for hunting, raiding other settlements, or seeking to trade with other groups.

their loved ones. The group chose to send Geronimo, the one who had suffered the greatest loss, to meet with other Apache tribes in hopes of getting them to join the war party.

Geronimo's story touched many, and they were eager to join the cause. Among the great leaders ready to fight were Cochise and Geronimo's old friend Juh, who had become the Nednai chief.

Geronimo and his band of Apache warriors were fierce fighters.

When the warriors assembled, they chose the Mexican city of Arizpe, in the state of Sonora, as their point of attack. The people of Arizpe became aware of the Apache presence outside of town. Frightened, the community members chose eight men to go out and talk with them. The Apache, however, had no intention of talking. They were there for revenge. As the town representatives drew near, the Apache killed them.

The next day, Mexican troops marched out to take on the native people, but the fighting wasn't intense. The two sides seemed to be trying to discover the other's intention. Once in a while, a gunshot would ring out or an arrow would fly. In spite of the lackluster battle, the Apache scored a huge victory. The troops had brought with them their supply train—a group of mules carrying extra ammunition and supplies, including food. When Apache warriors captured the supply train, the soldiers lost all hope that the Indians would just go away.

Cochise was one of the Apache leaders ready to fight the Mexicans with Geronimo.

The Mexican commander needed to do something to gain back his advantage and decided to bring out the full force of his troops. He called in the cavalry to aid the soldiers who stood ready at the scene. This proved to be the move the Apache desired. The Indians believed these very cavalrymen were the ones who had slaughtered their families in Janos.

In a bold move, Geronimo asked to be named war chief for the battle. Though still young and inexperienced as a leader, he had lost more in Janos than the others. The chiefs recognized this and named Geronimo war chief out of respect for his suffering. "I was no chief and never had been, but because I had been more deeply wronged than others, this honor was conferred upon me, and I resolved to prove worthy of the trust," Geronimo said.

As the Mexican soldiers started shooting, the Apache warriors charged. Geronimo poured all his anger and hatred into the fight. When he used all his arrows, he grabbed his deadly spear. He fought so fiercely that the Mexicans' eyes were drawn to him. They started yelling "Geronimo," the Spanish word for Jerome. The reason for this has been lost over time, but some

Born in northern Italy in about 340, Saint Jerome was a doctor and priest. When barbarians attacked Rome in 410, Jerome found safe shelter for many Roman Christians.

*Geronimo's pos
sible namesake,
Saint Jerome,
translated the
Bible from Greek
and Hebrew
into Latin.*

believe the Mexicans might have been shouting to
Saint Jerome. Whatever the reason, the warrior
Goyakla forever became known as Geronimo that
day, and the Apache secured their revenge.

4 THE WHITE INVASION

❧

After two hours of intense, bloody fighting, the battle-field outside of Arizpe was covered with bodies. Both sides suffered many losses, but the Mexicans had lost more. They retreated to Arizpe. The Apache considered this a victory and headed back to their own camps.

But Geronimo had other plans. He'd fallen in love with a woman named Chee-hash-kish and went to claim her as his wife. According to Apache custom, Geronimo was expected to live with her people in the Dragoon and Chiricahua mountains of south-eastern Arizona. Once there, Geronimo found himself under the leadership of Cochise. A well-known and respected chief, Cochise stood 6 feet 2 inches (188 centimeters) tall, a giant among the Apache

Artist Frederick Remington created this image of Geronimo and his band returning from a raid in Mexico.

people. The sturdy, square-jawed Geronimo only stood about 5 feet 9 inches (175 cm) tall.

Between the Dragoon and Chiricahua mountains lay Apache Pass, which was quickly becoming an important path for white Americans heading west to Tucson and California. While this route sat in the heart of Apache country, other, less hostile paths lacked the one thing that made Apache Pass most attractive—water. Cochise kept the path open, but never promised anyone safe passage.

He never promised the Mexicans that raids on their communities would stop either, much to the embarrassment of the U.S. government. Raids on

A cavalry patrol leaves Fort Bowie. The fort was built in 1862 near Apache Pass.

Sonora continued, and Geronimo conducted many of them himself.

While the battle at Arizpe quenched many warriors' thirsts for revenge, Geronimo still felt hatred toward the Mexicans and wanted them to suffer more pain. He made plans for another raid and secured the help of two other warriors—Ah-koch-ne and Ko-deh-ne.

> *In 1862, the U.S. military established Fort Bowie to try to help protect American travelers making their way through Apache Pass.*

The three warriors sneaked into a Sonoran town early in the morning. Seeing five horses grouped together, the men decided to steal them. As they crept toward their goal, they believed they were unobserved—until a rain of gunfire came from nearby buildings. Ah-koch-ne and Ko-deh-ne died in the hail of bullets. Geronimo found himself with no other option than to run for his life.

The Sonorans chased Geronimo, but his skill at hiding kept him safe. In the days it took him to return home, he lived like a fugitive. Having used all his arrows, he only carried a knife for protection. He feared falling asleep and being discovered, so he forced himself to stay awake.

By the time he arrived home, Geronimo was exhausted and hungry. When he showed up without Ah-koch-ne and Ko-deh-ne, he didn't receive a warm welcome.

Some of the Apaches blamed me for the evil result of the exhibition, but I said nothing. Having failed, it was only proper that I should remain silent. But my feelings toward the Mexicans did not change—I still hated them and longed for revenge. I never ceased to plan for their punishment, but it was hard to get the other warriors to listen to my proposed raids.

In another Mexican raid, Geronimo almost lost his life. After slipping in a pool of blood, Geronimo felt the butt of a gun slam into his head. He fell to the ground unconscious. When the battle ended, the Apache looked for injured friends who could be saved. They found Geronimo and helped him to his feet. Despite his injuries, Geronimo made it back to camp without any more help, but he carried the scar for the rest of his life. "In this fight we had lost so heavily that there really was no glory in our victory, and we returned to Arizona," Geronimo remembered. "No one seemed to want to go on the warpath again that year."

As time went on, Geronimo decided to move his family farther north and join Mangas Coloradas and the Warm Springs band. Geronimo's family now included two wives, Chee-hash-kish and Nana-tha-thtith, and the

Nana-tha-thtith and her child were killed by Mexican troops in the early 1850s. Their deaths further fueled Geronimo's hatred of Mexicans.

children he had with them—a son, Chappo, and daughter, Dohn-say, with Chee-hash-kish and one more child with Nana-tha-thtith. Apache men could marry as many women as they were able to support. Having more than one wife was a symbol of prosperity.

Heading north, however, did not take them away from trouble with whites. Unlike the whites heading through Apache Pass who never planned to stay, the whites coming to the land near the Warm Springs band had no intention of leaving.

Chappo, the son of Geronimo

What drew them to the area were rich deposits of silver, copper, and other minerals. Because the miners hoped the deposits would make them rich, they cared little for the rights of the Indians who lived on the land. The Apache responded by killing travelers in the area. Still, the miners wouldn't leave.

In 1860, gold was discovered, and the town of Pinos Altos (now in the state of New Mexico) sprang up. The U.S. Army founded Fort McLane nearby to help keep peace between the miners and Indians.

Meanwhile, the U.S. government was busy preparing plans to move Indian tribes in the Southwest onto smaller reservations, leaving the remaining land open to white development and settlement.

In an effort to build a peaceful relationship, Mangas Coloradas went on a friendly visit to the Pinos Altos miners' camp in 1860. Despite the warnings of Geronimo and other Warm Springs leaders, Mangas still believed peace was possible between his people and the miners.

After Mangas entered the camp, however, the miners tied him to a tree and whipped him. Eventually he escaped and vowed revenge for the way he was treated. Beginning in late September 1860, no white settlement or supply train was safe. The chiefs and their warriors killed travelers, burned wagons, and captured livestock. The white miners fought back by attacking the Apache camps.

In 1861, Geronimo was back living with the Chiricahua. There he married a relative of Cochise named She-gha. He also took another wife named Shtsha-she. While he participated in raids to chase whites out of the area, his focus remained making the Mexicans pay for the suffering they had caused him.

In 1861, Cochise met with U.S. Army Lieutenant George Bascom who accused him of kidnapping a Mexican boy and stealing livestock. Believing the meeting would be a friendly one, Cochise had brought with him his wife and child and his brother and two nephews. Though Cochise protested his innocence, Bascom, a young officer hungry to make a name for himself, told Cochise that he and his people would remain hostages until the boy and the livestock were returned.

George Bascom was a 24-year-old, inexperienced Army lieutenant when he was sent to investigate the kidnapping and livestock theft believed to be the work of Cochise and his followers.

Rather than be taken prisoner for something he didn't do, Cochise beat a hasty exit, cutting a hole in the tent where he was meeting with Bascom and running off. Surprised by Cochise's sudden move, the soldiers couldn't catch him. One of Cochise's nephews tried to escape as well, but the soldiers were ready this time. They clubbed him and stabbed him with a bayonet. The others were trapped.

Wanting his family returned safely, Cochise secured four American hostages of his own. He told Bascom he'd exchange the Americans for his relatives. When Bascom refused to negotiate, Cochise killed his prisoners. Bascom responded by hanging Cochise's brother and nephews, though his wife and child were eventually released.

In January 1863, tragedy also struck the Warm Springs band. Geronimo and his family were living with them again, under Mangas Coloradas' leadership.

> *The deaths of Cochise's brother and nephews sparked an 11-year war between the Apache and the whites who dared venture into the American Southwest.*

Mangas was ready to talk peace despite Geronimo's warning not to trust the whites. As a compromise, Mangas agreed to take half the band with him to talk peace at Fort McLane in the Territory of New Mexico. The remaining Apache would stay at camp under Geronimo's leadership and await word from Mangas.

Pretending they wanted a truce, a group of soldiers and some miners from Pinos Altos lured Mangas from the rest of the group. They captured the chief, then tortured and killed him. Soldiers massacred the Apache who had journeyed with him. Geronimo awaited news from Mangas. If the whites proved true to their words, Geronimo would lead the rest of the band to join Mangas and the others.

> *No word ever came to us from them. From other sources, however, we heard that they had been treacherously captured and slain. In this dilemma we did not know just exactly what to do, but fearing that the troops who had captured them would attack us, we retreated into the mountains near Apache Pass.*

After Mangas' death, Geronimo gained power. Mangas had trusted the whites and paid with his life.

Geronimo's distrust of the soldiers proved to be valid. The elders of the tribe started seeking out Geronimo's opinions and valued his thoughts. While the United States now proved itself the enemy of the Apache, Geronimo still concentrated mostly on Mexico. His hatred toward the Mexicans never waned. ✑

Geronimo holds an Apache council meeting.

5 SAN CARLOS

Chapter

ᥒᥣᥴ᥍᥍ᥲᥣ

From 1861 to 1865, the United States was embroiled in a bloody Civil War. When the war ended, the U.S. government could once again concentrate its efforts on settling the American Southwest. This meant spending more time dealing with Indian issues.

U.S. policy for dealing with the Indians flip-flopped many times—it changed depending on who had the most power in Washington, D.C. The leadership skills of agents sent to deal with the issue in the Southwest also played a role in how policy was carried out. Over the years, the policy ranged from planned round-ups of Indians onto reservations to their extermination—and everything in between.

In the mid-1870s, the San Carlos Reservation in southwestern Arizona was chosen as the one place

The U.S. government's efforts to settle the American Southwest were put on hold while its military fought to preserve the Union during the Civil War.

where many of the Indians from the Southwest would be settled. American policy leaned toward establishing one reservation for all Indians living in Arizona and southwest New Mexico. Creating just one reservation would cut down on administrative costs, some white leaders said. In reality, the whites' call for one reservation likely had more to do with keeping more land for white settlements, mining, and other uses than for saving the government money.

Establishing just one reservation created additional hardships for the Indians. Some of the tribes had been warring with one another. But the government didn't care. Now that they were living together, all the Indians were expected to cease their previous hostilities and live in peace.

By 1876, 4,200 Indians of various tribes were living at San Carlos. In June 1876, when Geronimo and his people were told it was time for them to join the reservation, they fled. This would be the first of many times Geronimo would lead his people into the mountains of Mexico before losing his freedom.

While a free man, Geronimo continued raiding Mexican towns. Finally in early 1877, the commissioner of Indian Affairs ordered that Geronimo and his followers be arrested and brought to San Carlos. There they would be jailed on charges of robbery and murder.

John Philip Clum (center) was appointed the Indian agent at the San Carlos Reservation in February 1874 and served until July 1877. He is surrounded by Apache scouts.

The man in charge of bringing Geronimo to justice was John Philip Clum. By tricking Geronimo into believing he only wanted to meet for a conference, Clum gained the distinction of being the only person ever to capture Geronimo. "The messengers did not say what they wanted with us, and as they seemed friendly we thought they wanted a council and rode in to meet the officers," Geronimo recalled.

Geronimo and his followers brought their wives and children to meet Clum and his men. After their arrival, Clum told Geronimo he intended to jail him and his warriors, not only for their refusal to stay at San Carlos, but for killing men and stealing livestock.

Geronimo replied, "We are not going to San Carlos with you, and unless you are very careful, you and your Apache police will not go back to San Carlos either. Your bodies will stay here at Ojo Caliente to make food for coyotes."

> *Some of the Apache who surrendered and agreed to live on reservations found work aiding the white leadership. They served in many capacities, including as scouts and policemen.*

But Geronimo was wrong. After listening to Geronimo speak, Clum motioned for his soldiers and Apache policemen to come out of their hiding places. Geronimo and his people were trapped. Clum personally grabbed Geronimo's rifle while others took the guns from the remaining Indian leaders. The rest of the group peacefully laid their weapons on the ground.

After the three-week journey to San Carlos, Geronimo and 18 other Apache were shackled and thrown into the guardhouse. The rest of Geronimo's people were told to set up camp on the reservation. Life at San Carlos proved miserable for the Apache. Not only had they lost their freedom, they were also exposed to new diseases, such as smallpox, which claimed many lives.

As Geronimo suffered in chains, Clum did all he could to ensure that the Apache warrior and his fellow prisoners would be hanged. In a letter to the

Tucson sheriff, Clum wrote: "I have personal evidence against some of these prisoners, and will be glad to testify against them. Through my Apache police, and information they have obtained … ample evidence is now available to convict each of the seven chiefs on many counts of murder."

Clum held Geronimo responsible for the deaths of more than 100 people and felt the leader's death would save the lives of countless others.

Clum didn't get his wish, however. Frustrated by the lack of appreciation he felt from the U.S. government, he eventually resigned from his job and was

A group of Apache women on horseback at San Carlos Reservation.

replaced by Henry Lyman Hart. Not having a history with Geronimo, Hart felt no ill will toward the Apache and released him. Geronimo later recalled:

> I was kept a prisoner for four months, during which time I was transferred to San Carlos. Then I think I had another trial although I was not present. In fact I do not know that I had another trial, but I was told that I had, and at any rate I was released. After this we had no more trouble with the soldiers, but I never felt at ease any longer at the Post. ... All went well for a period of two years, but we were not satisfied.

During that time, white agents had come and gone. Some proved honest and helpful, while others were corrupt. Some even filled their pockets by selling supplies meant for those living on the reservation.

Disease continued to plague the Indians, as did lack of food and decent clothing. They began stealing weapons in preparation for their escape from this dismal life. On April 4, 1878, Geronimo gathered his family and friends and broke away from the reservation. Joining with his friend Juh, Geronimo led his people into the Sierra Madres where they may have lived in fear of being captured again, but at least they were free.

John Clum's problem with the U.S. government partly revolved around money. He believed he deserved a raise for all the money he had saved the country by combining five Indian reservations into just one—San Carlos. He also started out in charge of 800 Indians, but that number grew to 5,000 with consolidation of the reservations. When no raise was offered, Clum quit.

Chapter
6 A SERIES OF FLIGHTS

⤐⧽⧼⤏

Not every Apache loved and respected Geronimo. A number of Apache blamed him for some of the troubles and deaths that had occurred. At Fort Apache (in modern-day Arizona), for example, most of the Indians peacefully tended to their crops and raised sheep and cattle. When Geronimo arrived, he often stirred up trouble and encouraged others to take off with him into the mountains. According to Samuel Kenoi, the son of one of Geronimo's men:

> *Pretty soon he would raid a settlement here, or kill a person, and the whole tribe would be blamed for it. Instead of coming and getting his rations and settling down and trying to be civilized, he would be out there like a wild animal, killing and raiding.*

An Apache woman carries her infant in a cradleboard near Fort Apache in 1873.

Then they would organize the Chiricahua scouts and send them out after Geronimo's men. In this way he caused Apache to fight Apache and all sorts of trouble to break out among our people.

Geronimo became a hunted man, and the U.S. government spent millions of dollars in resources

Artist Frederick Remington's drawing of Native American scouts hunting for Geronimo along the Mexican border appeared on the cover of Harper's Weekly *in 1886.*

and manpower to bring him into captivity. Those Chiricahua scouts would help lead the way.

Along with being hunted by Americans, Geronimo and his band were chased by the Mexicans. In one attack, Geronimo's wife Chee-hash-kish was taken prisoner by Mexican troops. With the loss of Chee-hash-kish, Geronimo took another wife, a Nednai called Zi-yeh.

The Chiricahua scouts were later treated like criminals and held captive with other Apache despite their years of service to the U.S. military.

Through the years, Geronimo developed a pattern of running free and raiding, then coming onto the reservations when times got tough or rations were being passed out. To some he was a hero, a man who lived according to his own rules. To others, he was a savage killer. Eventually, the U.S. government grew tired of his comings and goings and decided to bring him in once and for all.

General George Crook was charged with the task of heading into Mexico to capture the renegade and his band. In 1883, Crook accomplished his task—but it was only the first time he would do so.

With a crew of 42 soldiers, 193 Apache scouts, nine officers, 266 mules, and 76 men in charge of the animals and the supplies they carried, Crook left for Mexico on May 1. They journeyed through barren lands in search of Geronimo and his people.

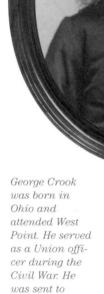

George Crook was born in Ohio and attended West Point. He served as a Union officer during the Civil War. He was sent to Arizona in 1882 to round up Geronimo and his followers.

"For three days we did not see a human being," Crook said. "The whole country had been laid waste by the Apaches and much land of value and for- merly cultivated had grown into a jungle of cane and mesquite."

People living in the communities that Crook passed on his journey lived in fear. They warmly greeted the men they hoped would capture Geronimo and the other Apache living in the area. "The condition of these little Mexican communities was deplorable," he said. "Apache attacks were to be looked for at any moment."

When he finally caught up with Geronimo, Crook listened to his story. Geronimo said he, too, wanted peace but the terrible conditions at San Carlos had led him and the others to flee. He admitted to attacking Mexican communities but explained the cause of his hatred toward that country's people. Crook also held Geronimo responsible for raids in the United States and the deaths of Americans, but Geronimo held firm to his statement that he killed only Mexicans.

Geronimo agreed to return to the United States

and try reservation life again. Back at San Carlos, Geronimo and his people lived on a beautiful stretch of land. Unfortunately, the land proved to be less than desirable as farmland, but Geronimo did his best for a while, raising a variety of produce.

Geronimo never completely trusted the whites running the reservation, though. It took only a rumor of trouble and a hint that he might again be chained and imprisoned to cause Geronimo to flee to freedom south of the American border. After another escape, Geronimo returned to the reservation in 1884, only to flee again the following year.

During one of his escape attempts, Geronimo's

Beef was distributed to the Indians living on the San Carlos Reservation. Living conditions on the reservation were very poor, and the land was not good for farming.

wives and several of his children were captured by American troops. Geronimo then took another wife, a Mescalero woman named Ih-tedda, whom he stole from her tribe.

By November 1885, the U.S. government, which continued to blame Geronimo for raids on American soil, sent Crook out again to bring the Apache under control. In March 1886, Crook met with Geronimo in Sonora and gave him a choice. He could either come back to the reservation peacefully or die fighting. "You must make up your own mind whether you will stay out on the warpath or surrender unconditionally," Crook said. "If you stay out, I'll keep after you and kill the last one, if it takes fifty years."

On March 27, Geronimo formally surrendered. The following day, Crook took off for the United States. He left an officer named Marion Maus behind with troops to bring the Indians to Fort Bowie in southeastern Arizona.

Maus found trouble right away. The night before, a bootlegger named Tribolett got the Apache group drunk. He didn't want them to leave. A smuggler as well as a bootlegger, Tribolett traded with the Apache raiders and didn't want to see his business come to an end. It is likely that he convinced Geronimo and several others that they were better off running and hiding than going back to the reservation. Even under normal circumstances,

Many U.S. soldiers—including Marion Maus (right) and Nelson Miles (second from left)—were involved in trying to round up Geronimo and his followers. William "Buffalo Bill" Cody (left) and Frank Baldwin are also pictured.

Geronimo wouldn't need much convincing. He and a small group took off.

Maus gave an officer and several scouts instructions to follow the original plan and head to Fort Bowie with the Apache who hadn't fled. Maus went after Geronimo and the others.

When word arrived at Fort Bowie that Geronimo was on the loose again, Crook asked to be relieved of his duties. Brigadier General Nelson A. Miles replaced him and set out to prove he could do what no one else had ever done—bring in Geronimo and keep him from ever leaving again. ◈

7 FINAL SURRENDER

∽⟨∾⟩∾

General Miles got right to work. He had 5,000 soldiers at his disposal—about one-fourth of the entire U.S. Army—to capture Geronimo and his band of 17 Apache.

Miles' first efforts involved the use of the cavalry, but he quickly learned that using horses in mountainous country wasn't a wise move. Meanwhile, Geronimo kept up his raids.

In July 1886, Miles sent Lieutenant Charles B. Gatewood to secure Geronimo's surrender. With the help of Chiricahua scouts, Gatewood followed Geronimo's trail in Mexico.

The mission proved a delicate one. Not only did Gatewood worry about finding Geronimo and not being killed in the process, he also had to avoid

Nelson A. Miles volunteered to serve in the Union Army during the Civil War. In 1886, he was sent to replace George Crook in the quest to capture Geronimo.

Mexican authorities who didn't want Americans coming into their country in search of Geronimo. The Mexicans planned to massacre the Apache on their own.

When Gatewood's scouts—Kaitah and Martine, who were also Apache—discovered Geronimo and his people in their rocky hideaway, they warned the group that their only options were surrender or death.

Geronimo (right) stands with some members of his tribe in 1886.

"All of you are my friends, and some of you are my brothers-in-law," Kaitah said. "I think a lot of you Indians, and I don't want you to get killed. The

troops are coming after you from all directions, from all over the United States. You people have no chance whatever. The War Department's aim is to kill every one of you if it takes fifty years to hunt you down. But if you people come as the government wants you to do, they will not harm you at all."

On August 23, a scout reported to Gatewood that he'd found Geronimo's people in the Torres Mountains about four miles (6.4 km) away. The lieutenant recalled:

Apache scouts who assisted in the hunt for Geronimo were mustered into the U.S. Army at a train station on the Great Plains.

> *[The scouts] had both been up there & had delivered General Miles' message, & Geronimo had sent one back to say that he would talk with me only, & that he was rather offended at our not coming straight to his rancheria, where peaceably inclined people were welcome. [Naiche], who was the real chief, if there was one, sent word that we would be perfectly safe so long as we behaved ourselves.*

The next morning, Gatewood traveled to Geronimo's camp. Geronimo said he'd surrender if he and his people were allowed to go back to their farms on the reservation and not be punished. He also asked that they be given rations, clothing, and tools for farming. Though Gatewood thought Geronimo's terms seemed fair, he couldn't say so. General Miles hadn't granted Gatewood the power to offer such concessions. "If I was authorized to accede to these modest propositions, the war might be considered at an end right there," Gatewood later admitted.

What Gatewood could offer was a trip to Fort Bowie and a chance to reunite with family members already captured. Gatewood warned Geronimo that if he didn't accept Miles' terms, fighting would likely continue. If the Apache wanted to surrender in the future, terms might never be this good again. Geronimo said he wanted to talk to General Miles before he'd surrender.

It is estimated that the U.S. government spent about $12 million to hunt down Geronimo and secure his final surrender.

On September 3, 1886, Miles arrived at Skeleton Canyon (near the border between Arizona and New Mexico) and met with Geronimo. Miles told him that he and his people would be sent to Florida but at least they'd be together. "Lay down your arms

Apache prisoners at Fort Bowie in mid-1880s

and come with me to Fort Bowie, and in five days you will see your families now in Florida … and no harm will be done you," Miles said. He also promised that Geronimo's past crimes would be forgotten.

After a night to think about his options, Geronimo surrendered. "I will quit the warpath and live at peace hereafter," Geronimo said.

Miles detailed the hunt for Geronimo in his report to Washington, D.C.:

Geronimo and
other Apache
prisoners were
guarded by
soldiers at Fort
Bowie in 1886.

*The hostiles fought until the bulk of their
ammunition was exhausted, pursued for
more than 2,000 miles over the most
rugged and sterile districts of the Rocky
and Sierra Madre Mountain regions,
beneath the burning heat of midsummer,*

until, worn down and disheartened, they
find no place of safety in our country or
Mexico, and finally lay down their arms
and sue for mercy from the gallant officers
and soldiers, who, despite every hardship
and adverse circumstance, have achieved
the success their endurance and fortitude
so richly deserved.

On September 5, Geronimo made the trip to Fort Bowie. Along the journey, he pointed out to Miles that this marked the fourth time he surrendered. "And I think it is the last time," Miles replied. Geronimo didn't realize it then, but he would spend the rest of his life as a prisoner. &

8 Chapter

CAPTIVITY

၍ᄋᢙᄋᢙᄋ

As the Apache group boarded the train bound for Florida on September 8, 1886, a military band played "Auld Lang Syne." As the song of farewell played, several soldiers broke out into laughter. The Apache just looked at them, not understanding the joke.

The whole experience was overwhelming for the native people. Many had never seen a train before, let alone traveled across the country in one. As the whistle blew on the train's approach to the station near Fort Bowie, many of the children hid in fear.

They were right to be afraid. Nearly 400 Indians were packed into 10 train cars. The windows and doors were shut tight to prevent anyone from escaping. The hot, smelly cars became a breeding ground for disease. Many Indians became infected with

Geronimo was captured in 1886 and remained a prisoner for the rest of his life.

tuberculosis while suffering on the long train ride.

The U.S. government quickly forgot Miles' promises to the Apache. Their families remained separated. Geronimo and several of the other Apache who were considered criminals began their train journey on September 8. The others didn't leave until September 13.

Geronimo and his fellow prisoners were stalled in San Antonio, Texas. Their future lay in the hands of President Grover Cleveland, who decided to honor at least part of Miles' agreement with the Apache. While Cleveland agreed to let them all live, Geronimo and the others who were considered criminals were sent to Fort Pickens, Florida. The rest of the group stayed in Fort Marion, Florida, about 300 miles (483 km) away on the east coast of Florida. The promise of a reservation where they could all live together was completely forgotten.

Secretary of War William Endicott justified the change in plans when he sent instructions on what to do with the Apache:

Grover Cleveland served as president of the United States from 1885 to 1889 and again from 1893 to 1897.

By direction of the President it is ordered that the hostile Apache adult Indians ... be sent under proper guard to Fort Pickens, Florida, there to be kept in close custody until further orders. These Indians have been guilty of the worst crimes known to the law ... and the public safety requires that they should be removed far from the scene of their [crimes] and guarded with the strictest vigilance. The remainder of the band captured at the same time, consisting of eleven women, six children, and two enlisted scouts, you are to send to Fort Marion, Florida, and place with other Apache Indians recently conveyed to and now under custody at that post.

Completed in 1834, Fort Pickens was on the western edge of Santa Rosa Island, just off the coast of the Florida Panhandle. Fort Pickens was one of several forts built to fortify Pensacola Harbor.

Geronimo was still in San Antonio when his wife Ih-tedda gave birth to their daughter Lenna at Fort Marion on September 13, 1886. It would be a long time before he learned of her birth or heard any news of his family.

At Fort Marion, attempts were made to Americanize the Indians. Children were forced to leave their parents and attend school. Samuel Kenoi was one of those children. "In the morning they strung out those poor children, and without trying to dress them up ... they sent them to the Catholic

William Endicott served as secretary of war from 1885 to 1889.

school in the city," he remembered. "They wore their loin cloths, wore rags around their heads, and were bare-legged."

James Kaywaykla also was one of those students, but his memories of those days at school were warmer. "[The] Catholic Sisters undertook to teach the children a little English, and provided baths, clothing, and sometimes medicine," he said. "I will never forget the kindness of those good women, nor the respect in which we held them. For the first time in my life I saw the interior of a church and dimly sensed that the White Eyes, too, worshipped Ussen."

Yet life at Fort Marion remained a nightmare by anyone's standards. Disease and lack of food ravaged the Indians. As the conditions at Fort Marion became more widely known, the public expressed outrage. The public outcry brought change, but it came slowly.

In 1887, the War Department decided to allow those Apache at Fort Marion who had family at Fort Pickens to join them there. On April 27, Geronimo finally met his daughter Lenna and was reunited with his wives. On September 28, though, Geronimo's wife She-gha succumbed to tuberculosis. It is likely she caught the disease while living at Fort Marion.

The Indians at Fort Marion who didn't have relatives at Fort Pickens were moved to Mount Vernon Barracks in Alabama. When these Apache arrived in Alabama, the man in charge, Major William Sinclair, couldn't believe his eyes. Many of the Indians were sick and hadn't had enough to eat for a very long time. Sinclair dared to speak up, saying it was horrifying that the Indians had to sell the few possessions

Before his capture, Geronimo lived in the southwestern United States and northern Mexico. After his capture, he and his followers were sent across the country to forts in the Southeast.

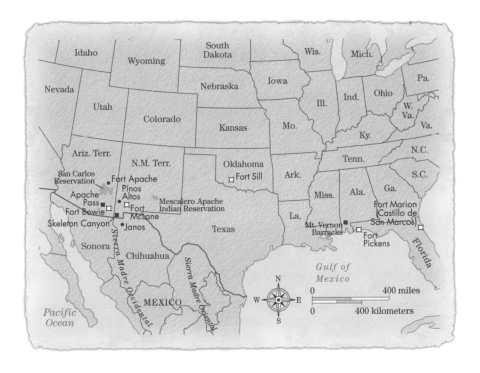

they had just to secure enough food to survive. "It is certainly a disgraceful condition of affairs ... when the prisoners are compelled to part with their private effects; the blankets required to keep them warm, and their crosses and other religious articles to obtain sufficient to eat," he wrote in one of his reports.

The Army finally responded by sending full military rations for the starving Apache. They also allowed the Indians to build small log cabins for shelter instead of making them live in tents. The log cabins included two rooms and dirt floors with no furniture, but they seemed like dream homes compared to conditions at Fort Marion.

Eventually, Geronimo and the Apache at Fort Pickens were shipped to Mount Vernon Barracks, too. Finally, they were all together again.

On Valentine's Day 1889, two teachers started a school for the Indian children right on the grounds where they lived. The children no longer had to be torn from their parents to go to a school where many of them felt like outcasts.

Geronimo understood the importance of getting an education in the world they now lived in. He made sure the children behaved and learned what their teachers were trying to share with them. Some of Geronimo's own children were students at the school.

Later that year, Geronimo faced a difficult decision. The Mescalero Apache asked that their people

Geronimo and some of his family members were living at Mount Vernon Barracks when this picture was taken in about 1890.

who had been caught up in the roundup of Geronimo and his people be sent back to New Mexico. The War Department agreed to let that happen. Geronimo's wife Ih-tedda was a Mescalero. Allowing her to go and take Lenna with her would be granting them freedom—something none of them enjoyed at Mount Vernon Barracks. Making the decision more heart-wrenching was the fact that Ih-tedda was pregnant. If Ih-tedda left, he might never see her or Lenna again, or ever meet the child she now carried. Yet Geronimo understood and cherished freedom. In reality, there was no choice.

> So many of our people died that I consented to let one of my wives go to the Mescalero Agency in New Mexico to live.

This separation is according to our custom equivalent to what the white people call divorce, and so she married soon after she got to Mescalero. She also kept our two small children, which she had a right to. The children, Lenna and Robbie, are still living in Mescalero, New Mexico.

This unselfish decision may have saved his children's lives. Robbie and Lenna were the only two of Geronimo's many children to live long enough to raise families of their own.

On October 4, 1894, Geronimo and the remaining Apache were moved again. This time, they found themselves at Fort Sill, Oklahoma. Geronimo was excited by the prospect of moving to a place where he could have a patch of land to farm.

I want to go somewhere where we can get a farm, cattle, and cool water. I have done my best to help the authorities—to keep peace & good order to keep my house clean. ... Young men old men women and children all want to get away from here— it is too hot and wet—too many of us die here. ... Every one of us have got children at school and we will behave ourselves on account of these children, we want them to learn. I do not consider that I am an Indian any more. I am a white man and [would] like to go around and see different places. I consider that all white men

*are my brothers and all white women are
my sisters—that is what I want to say.*

*Geronimo and
his family
farmed small
plots of land
at Fort Sill,
Oklahoma.*

While the Apache were able to claim their own little plots of land and raise crops and cattle, they couldn't shake the scourge of disease. Geronimo believed they'd never truly regain their health until they were allowed to go home, back to the Southwest. "We are vanishing from the earth," he said. "The Apaches and their homes each [were] created for the other by Usen himself. When they are taken away from these homes they sicken and die. How long will it be until it is said, there are no Apaches?" Despite his pleas, Geronimo and the other Apache at Fort Sill remained captive. ᴖ

Chapter
9   SIDESHOW

❧❧❧

At train stops from Fort Bowie to Florida, and again en route to Oklahoma, Army officials noticed all the attention Geronimo and the other Apache drew. People pushed and shoved to get a better view. Even at Fort Pickens, people lined up for the chance to see the caged Apache as if the Indians were animals in a zoo.

Many looked for ways to profit from the captive Apache. Geronimo quickly caught on and found ways to keep some of the profit for himself. In 1898, Geronimo was an attraction at the Trans-Mississippi and International Exhibition in Omaha, Nebraska. This was just the first of many similar appearances. Though still a guarded prisoner, Geronimo traveled the country, visiting fairs and exhibitions. He

While in captivity, Geronimo traveled the country appearing at fairs and exhibitions. Many people were eager to get a look at the infamous Indian.

*The 1904
World's Fair
in St. Louis,
Missouri, was
held to celebrate
the 100th
anniversary of
the Louisiana
Purchase. It
is sometimes
referred to as
the Louisiana
Purchase
Exposition.*

showed his skill at making bows and profited from selling what he made or by selling pictures and autographs. He even discovered the buttons of his coat held value to some people. For a price, he'd pluck off the buttons but always kept a supply with him to sew back on and sell to others.

In 1904, Geronimo was asked to appear as an attraction at the St. Louis World's Fair. He later recalled:

When I was at first asked to attend the St. Louis World's Fair I did not wish to go. Later, when I was told that I would receive good attention and protection, and that the President of the United States said that it would be all right, I consented. I sold my photographs for twenty-five cents, and was allowed to keep ten cents of this for myself. I also wrote my name for ten, fifteen, or twenty-five cents, as the case might be, and kept all of that money. I often made as much as two dollars a day, and when I returned I had plenty of money—more than I had ever owned before.

In 1905, Geronimo headed to Washington, D.C. President Theodore Roosevelt wanted the famous Indian to participate in his second inaugural parade. Geronimo understood the importance of the event and was excited about the invitation. His favorite horse was shipped to the capital for the special event.

While Geronimo thought his participation in the parade was a great honor, in truth, Roosevelt was just using the Apache. A newspaperman who sat by the president as he watched the parade in front of the White House, asked about Geronimo's participation. "To him I

The ice cream cone was one of the new inventions unveiled at the 1904 World's Fair. The fair was held in St. Louis, Missouri, from April 30 through December 1.

Geronimo was one of several Indian chiefs who rode in the parade celebrating the inauguration of President Theodore Roosevelt on March 4, 1905.

said, 'Why did you select Geronimo to march in your own parade, Mr. President? He is the greatest single-handed murderer in American history,'" the reporter recalled. "To which he characteristically replied, 'I wanted to give the people a good show.'"

Roosevelt may not have truly respected Geronimo,

but the old Apache respected the president. Geronimo even dedicated his autobiography to him.

> *Because he has given me permission to tell my story; because he has read that story and knows I try to speak the truth; because I believe that he is fair-minded and will cause my people to receive justice in the future; and because he is chief of a great people, I dedicate this story of my life to Theodore Roosevelt.*

Geronimo didn't realize the president and many other white Americans saw him as a sideshow attraction. 🪶

10 DEATH

⤲⦸⤵

Throughout his life, Geronimo had dealt with loss. When he lost his home and freedom, he spent the rest of his life trying to get back to the American Southwest. He told anyone who would listen that he wanted to go back to the land he loved. "I want to go back to my old home before I die," Geronimo told a newspaper reporter in 1908. "Tired of fight and want to rest. Want to go back to the mountains again. I asked the Great White Father [U.S. president] to allow me to go back, but he said no."

In his own way, Geronimo grieved for the wives and children he had lost to violence and disease. When his wife Zi-yeh contracted tuberculosis and died in 1904, Geronimo showed his domestic side. His beloved daughter Eva had been born in 1889,

Geronimo was skilled at making bows and arrows. He practiced this craft throughout his life.

Geronimo began to show his age in the early 1900s.

and he was determined to keep a nice home for her. Geronimo washed dishes, swept floors, and accomplished other household tasks.

But when Geronimo's beloved grandson Thomas died March 11, 1908, at the age of 18, he seemed to feel this loss more deeply. Thomas was the son of Geronimo's daughter Lulu. Within the first five years of living at Fort Sill, Lulu had died. Since then, Geronimo felt a special responsibility toward young Thomas, and the two had grown very close. Though he wasn't one for showing a lot of emotion, Geronimo was never the same after Thomas' death.

In the winter of 1908–1909, the strong, vital Geronimo finally started to show his age. Once one of the most feared men in the country, Geronimo now appeared to be a shell of his former self. His short muscular frame began to shrink, and he started to forget things. He also didn't live quite as active a life as he had in the past. One exception was making bows and arrows. He kept working on his craft, his fingers as nimble as ever.

Geronimo (in top hat) drives a car in Oklahoma in about 1908.

On February 11, 1909, Geronimo braved the cold and headed into Lawton, Oklahoma, to sell some of his bows and arrows. With the money he made, he bought some whiskey. Geronimo sought comfort in alcohol, but he didn't find it there. In fact, drinking led to his death.

Geronimo was drunk and decided to ride home from Lawton in the dark. Along the way, he fell off his horse and landed partly in a creek. He lay there until morning when a passerby discovered him.

After spending the night cold and wet, Geronimo developed pneumonia. Doctors doubted he would live long. Knowing the end was near, Geronimo asked that his surviving children be brought to Fort Sill to be with him in his final moments. Geronimo clung to life waiting for their arrival, but the Army surgeon had summoned them with a letter instead of a telegram. They didn't get to Fort Sill until the day of his funeral.

Geronimo's grave is located at Fort Sill, Oklahoma.

Geronimo died at 6:15 A.M. on February 17 with Apache friends at his bedside. He was 79. Geronimo

was buried at the Apache Cemetery at Fort Sill, Oklahoma, next to his wife Zi-yeh and other deceased family members.

Today, a large rock monument marks Geronimo's grave. A large eagle made of rock graces the top of the monument. A symbol of the freedom Geronimo treasured, it is a fitting marker for the final resting place of this famous warrior.

Many newspaper reporters sought interviews with Geronimo. The American public was fascinated by him. Many reporters, believing the legends that grew around Geronimo, asked to see a blanket they'd heard was made from the scalps of people he'd killed. No such blanket ever existed.

GERONIMO'S LIFE

1829

Born in June in
present-day
Arizona

1846

Becomes a warrior
after he turns 17
and marries his
first wife, Alope

1840

1840

Auguste Rodin,
famous sculptor of
The Thinker, is born

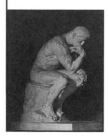

1829

The first practical
sewing machine is
invented by French
tailor Barthélemy
Thimonnier

1848

*The Communist
Manifesto* by German
writer Karl Marx is
widely distributed

WORLD EVENTS

1851

Geronimo's wife, Alope, their three children, and his mother are killed by Mexican troops in a March 5 massacre

1863

Mangas Coloradas, who fought with Geronimo, is murdered

1860

1850

Jeans are invented by Levi Strauss, a German who moved to California during the gold rush

1859

A Tale Of Two Cities by Charles Dickens is published

1863

Thomas Nast draws the modern Santa Claus for *Harper's Weekly*, although Santa existed previously

GERONIMO'S LIFE

1878

Is among a group of Apache that flee San Carlos on April 4 and run to the mountains of Mexico

1877

Geronimo and his family are captured; Geronimo is jailed at San Carlos

1876

Flees with his family to Mexico to avoid going to the San Carlos Reservation

1875

1876

Alexander Graham Bell uses the first telephone to speak to his assistant, Thomas Watson

1877

German inventor Nikolaus A. Otto works on what will become the internal combustion engine for automobiles

1879

Electric lights are invented

WORLD EVENTS

1886

Finally surrenders to
General Nelson A. Miles
at Skeleton Canyon
and is eventually sent
to Florida

1887

Sent to Mount
Vernon Barracks
in Alabama

1890

1886

Grover Cleveland
dedicates the Statue
of Liberty in New
York, a gift from the
people of France

1881

The first Japanese
political parties
are formed

GERONIMO'S LIFE

1894

Arrives with his
people in Fort Sill
in Oklahoma

1898

Is an attraction at
the Trans-Mississippi
and International
Exhibition in Omaha,
Nebraska, the first of
many similar events

1900

1896

The Olympic Games
are held for the first
time in recent history
in Athens, Greece

1893

Women gain voting
privileges in New
Zealand, the first
country to take
such a step

1901

Queen Victoria dies

WORLD EVENTS

1905

Rides in President
Theodore Roosevelt's
second term
inaugural parade

1906

Autobiography
is published

1909

Dies at Fort Sill on
February 17

1910

1903

Brothers Orville
and Wilbur Wright
successfully fly a
powered airplane

1909

The National
Association for the
Advancement of
Colored People
(NAACP) is founded
in the United States

NICKNAME: Geronimo (his given name was Goyakla)

DATE OF BIRTH: June 1829

BIRTHPLACE: Near the headwaters of the Gila River near the present-day city of Clifton, Arizona

FATHER: Taklishim

MOTHER: Juana

EDUCATION: No formal education

SPOUSES: First wife was Alope; subsequent wives included (though even he couldn't remember all their names): Chee-hash-kish, Nana-tha-thtith, She-gha, Shtsha-she, Zi-yeh, Ih-tedda, Sousche, and Azul

DATE OF MARRIAGES: Most of these dates were not documented, but he married Sousche December 25, 1905

CHILDREN: Geronimo had several children, but the names of only a few are known: Chappo, Dohn-say, Fenton, Eva, Lenna, Lulu, and Robbie.

DATE OF DEATH: February 17, 1909

PLACE OF BURIAL: Apache Cemetery, Fort Sill, Oklahoma

IN THE LIBRARY

Hermann, Spring. *Geronimo: Apache Freedom Fighter*. Springfield, N.J.: Enslow Publishers, 1997.

Schwarz, Melissa. *Geronimo: Apache Warrior*. New York: Chelsea House Publishers, 1992.

Stanley, George E. *Geronimo: Young Warrior*. New York: Aladdin Paperbacks, 2001.

Thompson, William. *Geronimo*. Philadelphia: Chelsea House Publishers, 2002.

LOOK FOR MORE SIGNATURE LIVES BOOKS ABOUT THIS ERA:

James Beckwourth: *Mountaineer, Scout, and Pioneer*

Crazy Horse: *Sioux Warrior*

Sam Houston: *Texas Hero*

Bridget "Biddy" Mason: *From Slave to Businesswoman*

Zebulon Pike: *Explorer and Soldier*

Sarah Winnemucca: *Scout, Activist, and Teacher*

ON THE WEB

For more information on *Geronimo*, use FactHound to track down Web sites related to this book.

1. Go to *www.facthound.com*
2. Type in a search word related to this book or this book ID: 0756510023
3. Click on the *Fetch It* button.

FactHound will find the best Web sites for you.

HISTORIC SITES

Arizona State Museum
University of Arizona
1013 E. University Blvd.
Tucson, AZ 85721-0026
520/621-6302
To learn more about the culture of Southwestern Indians

Fort Bowie National Historic Site
3203 S. Old Fort Bowie Road
Bowie, AZ 85605
520/847-2500
To learn more about the U.S. conflict with the Apache and the surrender of Geronimo

The National Museum of the American Indian
Fourth Street and
Independence Avenue Southwest
Washington, DC 20024
202/633-1000
To learn more about the Apache and other American Indian groups

annexed
added a territory to a country

aught
anything

bayonet
a long knife that can be placed on the end
of a rifle

cavalry
an army regiment mounted on horseback

chastised
scolded

consolidation
a large group made up of several smaller groups

corrupt
characterized by improper behavior and a lack
of morals

diplomatic
related to the relationships between countries

persevered
kept going, despite difficulties and opposition

prosperity
condition of being financially well-off

rancheria
small farm or ranch

renegade
a person who lives by his or her own rules

smallpox
a contagious disease recognized by the eruption
of pus-filled spots on an infected person's skin

sowed
caused

treacherously
in an untrustworthy manner

Chapter 1

Page 11, line 13: C. L. Sonnichsen. *Geronimo and the End of the Apache Wars*. Lincoln: University of Nebraska Press, 1990, p. 36.

Page 12, line 5, Ibid., p. 36.

Chapter 2

Page 18, line 12: Alexander B. Adams. *Geronimo*. New York: G.P. Putnam's Sons, 1971, p. 47.

Page 18, line 25: S. M. Barrett. *Geronimo's Story of His Life*. New York: Duffield & Company, 1907, p. 18-19.

Page 20, line 11: Angie Debo. *Geronimo: The Man, His Time, His Place*. Norman: University of Oklahoma Press, 1976, p. 24-25.

Page 21, line 12: *Geronimo*, p. 49.

Page 21, line 22: *Geronimo*, p. 49.

Page 22, line 11: *Geronimo's Story of His Life*, p. 25.

Page 23, line 14: *Geronimo: The Man, His Time, His Place*, p. 18.

Page 24, line 18: Ibid., p. 19.

Page 25, line 3: *Geronimo's Story of His Life*, p. 36-37.

Page 26, line 1: Ibid., p. 37-38.

Page 26, line 22: *Geronimo: The Man, His Time, His Place*, p. 31.

Page 27, line 1: Ibid., p. 32.

Chapter 3

Page 30, line 20: Ibid., p. 46.

Page 34, line 17: Ibid., p. 37.

Page 35, line 5: *Geronimo: The Man, His Time, His Place*, p. 38.

Page 38, line 17: *Geronimo's Story of His Life*, p. 52.

Chapter 4

Page 44, line 1: *Geronimo*, p. 101.

Page 44, line 18: *Geronimo: The Man, His Time, His Place*, p. 49.

Page 48, line 19: *Geronimo's Story of His Life*, p. 121.

Chapter 5

Page 53, line 5: *Geronimo: The Man, His Time, His Place*, p. 105.

Page 54, line 1: Ibid., p. 105.

Page 55, line 1: Ibid., p. 114.

Page 56, line 4, Ibid., p. 111.

Chapter 6

Page 59, line 10: *Geronimo and the End of the Apache Wars*, p. 72.

Page 62, line 1: *Geronimo: The Man, His Time, His Place*, p. 178.

Page 62, line 16: Ibid., p. 178.

Page 64, line 11: Ibid., p. 259.

Chapter 7

Page 68, line 9: *Geronimo and the End of the Apache Wars*, p. 76.

Page 69, line 20: Ibid., p. 60.

Page 70, line 9: Ibid., p. 62.

Page 70, line 28: *Geronimo: The Man, His Time, His Place*, p. 292.

Page 71, line 6: *Geronimo*, p. 306.

Page 72, line 1: Ibid., p. 298.

Page 73, line 12: Ibid., p. 293.

Chapter 8

Page 77, line 1: Ibid., p. 308.

Page 77, line 30: Ibid., p. 319.

Page 78, line 11: Ibid., p. 319.

Page 80, line 1: Ibid., p. 337.

Page 81, line 13: Ibid., p. 342.

Page 82, line 17: Ibid., p. 360-361.

Page 83, line 8: Ibid., p. 378.

Chapter 9

Page 87, line 1: *Geronimo's Story of His Life*, p. 197.

Page 87, line 30: *Geronimo and the End of the Apache Wars*, p. 119.

Page 89, line 3: *Geronimo's Story of His Life*, dedication page.

Chapter 10

Page 91, line 5: *Geronimo*, p. 313.

Adams, Alexander B. *Geronimo.* New York: G.P. Putnam's Sons, 1971.

Barrett, S.M. *Geronimo's Story of His Life.* New York: Duffield & Company, 1907.

Debo, Angie. *Geronimo: The Man, His Time, His Place.* Norman: University of Oklahoma Press, 1976.

Encyclopedia of American Indians Web site. Houghton Mifflin. http://college.hmco.com/history/readerscomp/naind/html/na_000107_entries.htm.

International Folklore Federation's World's Fair Centennial site. http://www.worldsfairstlouis.org/index.php.

Santee, Ross. *Apache Land.* Lincoln: University of Nebraska Press, 1971.

Sonnichsen, C. L. *Geronimo and the End of the Apache Wars.* Lincoln: University of Nebraska Press, 1990.

Brenda Haugen started in the newspaper business and had a career as an award-winning journalist before finding her niche as an author. Since then, she has written and edited many books, most of them for children. A graduate of the University of North Dakota in Grand Forks, Brenda lives in North Dakota with her family.

Image Credits